W9-AJL-809

Disasters Up Close

FLOODS

Michael Woods
and Mary B. Woods

Lerner Publications Company

MINNEAPOLIS

To Mary Kate Woods, with gratitude for her
wise counsel

Editor's note: Determining the exact death toll following disasters is often difficult—if not impossible—especially in the case of disasters that took place long ago. The authors and the editors in this series have used their best judgment in determining which figures to include.

Text copyright © 2007 by Michael Woods and Mary B. Woods

Lerner Publications Company
A division of Lerner Publishing Group
241 First Avenue North
Minneapolis, MN 55401 U.S.A.

Website address: www.lernerbooks.com

Library of Congress Cataloging-in-Publication Data

Woods, Michael, 1946–
    Floods / by Michael Woods and Mary B. Woods.
      p.   cm. — (Disasters up close)
    Includes bibliographical references and index.
    ISBN-13: 978-0-8225-4712-9 (lib. bdg. : alk. paper)
    ISBN-10: 0-8225-4712-0 (lib. bdg. : alk. paper)
    1. Floods—Juvenile literature. I. Woods, Mary B. (Mary Boyle), 1946–
  II. Title.
  GB1399.W66 2007
  363.34'93—dc22   2006023953

Manufactured in the United States of America
1 2 3 4 5 6 – DP – 12 11 10 09 08 07

Contents

Introduction

ANJALI KRISHNAN WAS DRIVING TO WORK ON JULY 26, 2005. SHE LIVED IN MUMBAI, INDIA. THIS CITY OF 13 MILLION PEOPLE WAS FORMERLY NAMED BOMBAY.

Floods cause traffic to stand still in Mumbai.

Rain began pouring down at 8:00 A.M. By 8:00 P.M., almost 37 inches (94 centimeters) had fallen in some places. Water collected on roads and streets. Creeks, rivers, and lakes overflowed. As the rain continued, the water got deeper and deeper.

Thousands of cars got stuck when water flooded the roads. People were stranded in their cars all day. By night many of them decided to walk home through the deep, swirling water.

Rain had flooded the buildings that usually collect and clean wastewater. So the floodwater was filled with sewage (wastes from toilet flushes). Dead animals were floating by. The animals had drowned in the flood. Krishnan had to wade through the filth for hours before reaching home.

But Krishnan was lucky. She lived through this terrible flood. At least 1,000 other people died. "For so many days we have been lifting the bodies of the dead and now we are clearing animals from the roads," said Hafeez Irani.

WATER DAMAGE

The flood covered land where almost 20 million people lived. Nearly 500,000 people had to be evacuated (moved to safer places). The high water flooded power plants that made electricity. Water also flooded plants that provided Mumbai with clean drinking water. "For the past seven days there has been no electricity nor drinking water," said Sikander Zhaid, who lived near Mumbai. "[Faucets] are churning out muddy and filthy water."

4

Without electricity, people had no lights. Refrigerators stopped working, and the food inside them rotted. There was no television or Internet service. People could not recharge their cell phones or music players. Without air-conditioning, people suffered in the heat and humidity.

When the water drained away, it left behind a huge mess. The rushing water had knocked down thousands of buildings. When water drained out of others, a thick layer of stinking mud remained. Walls, furniture, beds, and clothing were ruined. Slimy mold started growing on the wet things.

Cars and buses that had been under the water would not start. The flood washed away crops growing in farmers' fields. It drowned cows and other farm animals. All that damage had to be repaired. It cost almost $900 million to fix the damage from this flood.

"The water was black and greasy right up to our necks and swirled fast around our waists."

—Anjali Krishnan, describing her experiences during the 2005 flooding of Mumbai, India

People walk home through flooded Mumbai, India, in July 2005. The flooding followed the heaviest rainfall ever recorded on a single day in India.

What Is a Flood?

A FLOOD IS TOO MUCH WATER IN THE WRONG PLACE. THE WATER OFTEN COMES FROM HEAVY RAIN THAT MAKES RIVERS OVERFLOW. MELTING SNOW AND ICE ARE ANOTHER COMMON CAUSE OF FLOODS. FLOODING ALSO CAN OCCUR IN OTHER WAYS. STORMS CAN PUSH SEAWATER ONTO THE SHORE. DAMS (WALLS BUILT ACROSS RIVERS TO BLOCK SOME OF THE WATER) MAY BREAK. TSUNAMIS MAY SEND WALLS OF WATER OVER THE LAND. TSUNAMIS ARE OCEAN WAVES CAUSED BY EARTHQUAKES OR UNDERWATER LANDSLIDES.

If the floodwater is deep, it can cause a disaster. A disaster is an event involving great destruction. Throughout history, floods have caused terrible disasters. Some have involved small areas and only a few people. Others have affected thousands or millions of people.

Floods happen more often, last longer, and strike more places than many other kinds of disasters. For example, the Great Midwest Flood of 1993 hit nine states and lasted more than four months.

GOOD FLOODS?

Some floods were helpful in the past. For thousands of years, floods of the Nile River in Egypt deposited silt along the river's banks each summer. Silt is often very rich soil. It washes off the land and into rivers during rainstorms. When rivers flood, they sometimes return silt to the land. Silt from the Nile River helped farmers grow their crops.

As time passed, more people lived near the Nile. Property damage from flooding became a big problem. In 1970 Egypt finished building the Aswan High Dam across the Nile River. It stopped the Nile's summer floods. The dam slowly releases water year-round. Farmers can plant two crops each year instead of just one. But the dam stopped the Nile's deposits of rich silt. Farmers had to start using artificial fertilizers to get good harvests.

This ancient Roman tile mosaic from Palestrina, Italy, shows the yearly flooding of the Nile River in Egypt.

"I hope I never see such a flood again," said Bob Gieseke, whose home and farm were damaged. The 2004 tsunamis caused flood disasters in 12 countries.

ONE DISASTER LEADS TO ANOTHER

A flood can lead to other disasters that are worse than deep water. Floods kill crops and farm animals that provide food for people. Many people may die from starvation.

People also may get sick and die from diseases they catch from touching or drinking floodwater. Floodwater is filthy and carries many germs. About 1,200 people in Bangladesh, a country in Asia, drowned in a 1974 flood. Another 24,500 died later from starvation or disease.

WORST OF THE WORST

The worst natural disaster in recorded history was a flood along China's Yellow River in 1887. This river looks yellow because of yellow silt in its water. As the water flows, silt drops out and collects on the river floor. Over time, it makes the river flow higher.

People began building levees (raised banks of earth that prevent flooding) along the Yellow River 2,500 years ago. As the riverbed filled in with silt, the levees had to be built higher to keep up. By 1887 some of the levees—and the river behind them—towered above the rooftops of houses.

Heavy rain poured down for months in 1887, swelling the Yellow River. In September the levees broke. A foaming wall of water rushed across the land. Water 10 feet (3 m) deep covered an area bigger than the states of Rhode Island, Delaware, New Jersey, and Connecticut combined. At least 900,000 people drowned, and 2 million people lost their homes.

One flood of the Yellow River in China lasted for 13 years!

INCREASING DISASTER THREAT

Floods have caused disasters throughout history. Even before people learned to write, they told stories about deluges (great floods) that caused terrible disasters.

In the United States, floods kill an average of 80 people and cause about $5 billion in damage each year. Floods in other parts of the world affect millions of people.

Floods are frightening, and people don't forget them. "I remember as a child in the 1950 flood, seeing my 6-foot-3-inch [1.9 meters] father carrying things out of our restaurant in water reaching chest high," said Bev Anderson, the mayor of Darlington, Wisconsin.

People are learning ways to limit the damage caused by some kinds of disasters. But floods are becoming a greater danger. More people are moving near seashores and other areas where floods happen. When the water rises, these people and their belongings are in danger. Changing weather patterns also may be causing more rain and a greater risk of floods in some areas.

THE BOSTON MOLASSES FLOOD

A flood of water is bad enough. Can you imagine a flood of thick, gooey molasses? It happened in Boston on January 15, 1919.

A storage tank filled with 2.3 million gallons (8.7 million liters) of molasses exploded. A wave of molasses 15 feet (4.6 m) high swept through part of the city. The flood (left) drowned 21 people, smashed buildings, and filled basements. The sticky coating on streets sucked off people's shoes. Residents claim that for more than 30 years, this part of Boston smelled of molasses.

Floodwaters destroyed this road in Henniker, New Hampshire, in May 2006.

"It's a nightmare. *The house looked like everything had just floated to the surface and somebody had stirred it.* **It was complete mayhem."**

—Yetta Chin, whose home in Maine was destroyed during floods in 2006

1889
THE JOHNSTOWN FLOOD

The rainstorms that caused the flood in Johnstown, Pennsylvania, also flooded other cities. These people are boating down a flooded street in Washington, D.C.

The South Fork Dam near Johnstown, Pennsylvania, was built across the Little Conemaugh River. It held back a lake 65 feet (20 m) deep and 3 miles (5 kilometers) long. The dam needed repairs. It had been leaking for years. People often joked that one day the dam would break.

On May 31, 1889, the lake's water level was higher than usual due to heavy rains. Suddenly the dam burst. It released a wall of water 30 feet (9 m) high that roared and foamed down the valley. At the end of the valley was Johnstown, a city of 30,000 people.

About 20 million tons (18 metric tons) of water came rushing down toward Johnstown at 40 miles (64 km) per hour. That's almost as fast as cars on a highway. Carried along by the water were huge rocks, whole trees, and other debris. When the wall of water hit buildings, they smashed into pieces.

"With one great swoop over 3,000 houses of brick and of wood, hotels, stores, dwellings, factories all were sent crashing, tumbling, and floating down the roaring torrent," said M. Elizabeth Morgan, an eyewitness. *"Above the roar of the flood, the crash of falling timber, and the swirl of*

This woodcut shows the empty reservoir after the South Fork Dam burst, flooding Johnstown.

> ## The water rose and floated us until our heads nearly touched the ceiling.
> ### It was dark and the house was tossing every way.
>
> —Anna Fenn, who survived the 1889 Johnstown flood in Pennsylvania

rushing waters were heard the groans of the dying, the wails of the mangled, and the agonizing cries for help. . . ."

The wave swept through South Fork, Mineral Point, and other nearby towns. C. W. Linthicum was another eyewitness. *"This seething flood was strewn with timber, trunks of trees, parts of houses, and hundreds of human beings, cattle, and almost every living animal,"* he said. *"We counted 107 people floating by and dead without number. A section of roof came by on which were sitting a woman and a girl."*

After the flood hit Johnstown, Charles Pitcarin sent a message to his office in Pittsburgh: *"Johnstown is annihilated [totally destroyed]."* The flood carried hundreds of people, broken buildings, train cars, trees, and other wreckage downstream into a railroad bridge. Everything piled up there. Oil from the trains caught on fire, and the pile of wreckage burned. The Johnstown flood killed more than 2,200 people, destroyed almost 1,900 homes and stores, and caused $17 million in damage.

13

What Causes Floods?

WATER IS THE MAIN INGREDIENT FOR FLOODS. EARTH HAS ABOUT 326 MILLION CUBIC MILES (1,360 MILLION CUBIC KM) OF WATER. WE CAN SEE IT IN OCEANS, LAKES, RIVERS, AND ICE. SOME WATER, HOWEVER, IS NOT VISIBLE. IT IS UNDER THE GROUND OR IN THE AIR.

Water moves from place to place and changes its form in what is known as the water cycle. Sidewalks dry off after a rain because the liquid water evaporates. It changes into water vapor, a gas that goes into the air. The water vapor then condenses (changes) into tiny droplets of liquid water. Together, many water droplets form a cloud. Water from clouds falls back to the ground as rain, snow, or ice. In this way, Earth recycles its water. The total amount of water on Earth does not change very much.

WAR FLOOD

In 1938 the Japanese army invaded China. Chiang Kai-shek, China's leader, decided to fight back with a flood. He ordered his soldiers to blow up levees along the Yellow River. The flood did slow down the Japanese army. However, it also killed at least half a million people who lived along the river.

TOO MUCH WATER

The ground can soak up just so much water from rain or melted snow and ice. Extra water then runs off into streams, rivers, and lakes. Too much water will make them overflow their banks, causing a flood.

Some of the worst floods occur when heavy rain makes big rivers overflow. Hurricanes and tropical storms often supply the rain. In 2004 Tropical Storm Jeanne dumped 13 inches (33 cm) of rain on the island of Haiti. The resulting floods killed almost 2,000 people and destroyed 200,000 homes.

These vehicles were washed away by floodwaters when Tropical Storm Jeanne hit Haiti in September 2004.

As hurricanes move, they push along a wall of water called a storm surge. When a hurricane reaches land, the storm surge flows over the ground like a huge wave. It can cause terrible floods. In 1900 a hurricane storm surge killed more than 8,000 people in Galveston, Texas. Hurricane Katrina's storm surge flooded and destroyed much of the city of New Orleans, Louisiana, in 2005.

FLOODS IN A FLASH

Flash floods are the most dangerous kind of flood. They happen so fast that people may not have time to escape. Flash floods often occur in streams or rivers that don't seem dangerous. The Big Thompson River is usually only 2 feet (0.6 m) deep, but during a 1976 flash flood, it suddenly became 20 feet (6 m) deep.

Some of the worst flash floods have occurred near dams. Water backs up behind a dam, forming a reservoir (lake). Modern dams are very strong and safe. In the past, however, dams have burst and released huge amounts of water. In 1889 the flash flood from a broken dam near Johnstown, Pennsylvania, killed more than 2,000 people.

FLOODS AND FLOODPLAINS

Rivers are more than water flowing through a long, narrow channel in the ground. They also include land along both sides of the river. This land is called the floodplain.

A floodplain is a flat area (a plain) where floods occur. It is the river's land. Every once in a while, heavy rains make a river overflow its banks. The water flows onto the floodplain.

People, however, like to live and work on the river's land. The soil on floodplains is rich. The land offers a good view of the water. Factories built along a river can use it to ship their products.

In the United States, hundreds of cities and towns have been built on the Mississippi River's floodplain. Flood disasters occur when the river takes back its land. More than 70 towns on the Mississippi were completely underwater during the Great Midwest Flood of 1993.

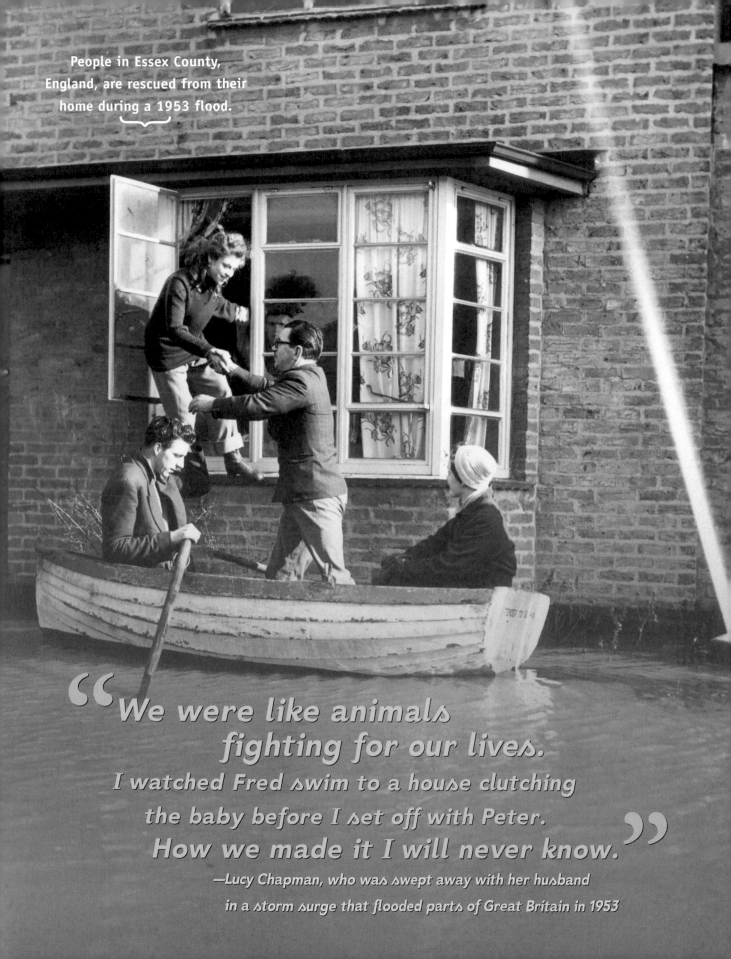

People in Essex County, England, are rescued from their home during a 1953 flood.

"We were like animals fighting for our lives. I watched Fred swim to a house clutching the baby before I set off with Peter. How we made it I will never know."

—Lucy Chapman, who was swept away with her husband in a storm surge that flooded parts of Great Britain in 1953

POWERFUL WATER

Water is soft and gentle when it's in a swimming pool. Water in a flood, however, is dangerous, because it flows with great force. Just 1 gallon (4 l) of water weighs about 8 pounds (nearly 4 kilograms). In a flood, billions of gallons of water flow very fast.

Alcutt McNaghten discovered what big objects floodwater can pick up. He was an eyewitness to the 1908 Great Folsom Flood in New Mexico. "The Wenger house and its four occupants was seen with the lights still burning floating down Grand Avenue and the screams of the occupants for help could be heard above the roar of the waters," he remembered.

The great Asian tsunami in 2004 knocked over a passenger train. It spun over and over four times. More than 800 passengers were killed.

TERRIBLE TSUNAMIS

Shock waves from earthquakes, volcanoes, and undersea landslides cause tsunamis. The shock waves travel through the open ocean like ripples in a swimming pool. They can pass right under a ship without causing any damage. When a tsunami reaches shallow water along the seashore, however, it rears up like a monster. The giant wave crashes over the land and causes great destruction.

A 1964 earthquake in Alaska produced tsunami waves 35 feet (11 m) high. They killed more than 120 people. In 1883 the Krakatau volcano in Indonesia erupted. It produced a wave of water so high that ships were carried more than 1 mile (1.6 km) inland.

Valdez, Alaska, was seriously flooded after a tsunami in 1964.

Powerful floodwaters during the 1889 Johnstown flood overturned this building and shoved a huge tree through it.

"It was so quick," said Danny Shahaf, a passenger, "it washed us so far away—the carriage [train car] kept filling up with water."

DANGER: SHALLOW WATER

In a flood, water 2 feet (0.6 m) deep can move with enough force to carry away a car. About half of all flood deaths in the United States happen when people try to drive cars through water that is deeper than it looks.

Just 6 inches (15 cm) of flowing water can knock a person down. People can be swept away into deeper water where they drown. They also may be hurt or killed when thrown against hard objects.

FIGHTING FLOODS WITH SAND

People often use cloth or plastic bags filled with sand to fight floods. They stack the sandbags to form walls. The walls keep water from flooding houses and other buildings. Sandbags also can be stacked on top of levees to make them higher.

Stacking sandbags is hard work. A properly filled sandbag weighs about 40 pounds (20 kg). It takes 2,000 bags to build a wall 100 feet (30 m) long. When the flood is over, the bags have to be removed. Then they're soaked with water and weigh even more.

During the Great Midwest Flood of 1993, people used 26.5 million sandbags to build walls to block off the water.

Rescuers fight the current to save a
person stranded by flooding in
Rockville, Maryland, in 1975.

YUCK!

Floodwater usually is filthy. It is loaded with dirt and germs. When city sewers overflow, floods pick up waste material that was flushed down toilets. One 1999 flood in North Carolina swept up 100 million gallons (380 million l) of hog manure.

When floods occur in poorer countries, there may be no clean water available. Then people must drink the floodwater. Many people who drink floodwater get sick, and some die.

When a flood ends, it leaves mud and slime behind. Dirt covers the ground and the floors and walls of buildings. Imagine spending days shoveling that muck out of your house. Dampness from flooding makes slimy, smelly mold grow on furniture, carpets, and walls. This mold can cause allergy attacks and make people sick in other ways.

A man and a woman scoop water out of a house during a 2003 flood in Xuyi, China.

Mold is growing on the walls and furniture in this house
in Chalmette, Louisiana. The building was damaged by
flooding caused by Hurricane Katrina in 2005.

1976
FLASH FLOOD: BIG THOMPSON RIVER

In 1976 a flash flood rushed down the Big Thompson Canyon in Colorado, washing out part of this cabin's foundation

July 31, 1976, was the last Saturday before the new school year started. Thousands of people were camping, hiking, or fishing along the Big Thompson River near Denver, Colorado. Many other people were nearby in homes, shops, motels, and restaurants.

The Big Thompson River flows through a beautiful 25-mile-long (40 km) canyon (a deep valley with walls rising almost straight up). Its water is only 2 feet (0.6 m) deep. Nobody dreamed that a thunderstorm would

change the gentle river into a monster.

Campers were cooking dinner when a thunderstorm began soaking everyone. Unlike most thunderstorms in the area, this storm did not move away quickly. It stayed over the Big Thompson Valley. In four hours, 1 foot (0.3 m) of rain fell. It ran off the hills, into the narrow canyon. Soon a 20-foot-high (6 m) wall of water was rushing down the canyon.

Lisa Wycoff, aged nine, was vacationing in a cabin with her family. At about 7:15 P.M., her mom opened the back door to check on the rain. *"She got out the flashlight, and found the river at our door,"* Wycoff remembered. *"It should've been 30 feet [9 m] away."*

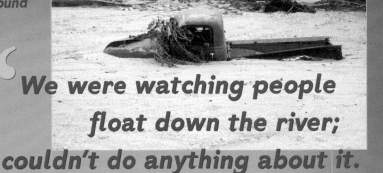

The water was rising fast. The Wycoffs could see that water already covered the hood of their car. Lisa started running

> ## We were watching people float down the river; couldn't do anything about it. At one time, one of the guys saw a bear floating down the river, just paddling away like mad.
>
> —Sheriff Robert Watson, describing the 1976 flash flood of the Big Thompson River

The floodwaters left a cabin perched on top of a bridge *(left)* and partly buried a pickup truck in sand *(above)*.

away from the river, followed by her father and, farther back, her mother and brother. *"I ran in ankle deep water,"* Lisa said. When she looked back, *"[the water] was knee high on my father. And, it was waist to chest high on my mom and brother. It was pitch black."*

Whole trees and rocks as big as cars tumbled through the water. They crushed everything in their path. Few people got any warning of the flood until they saw the wall of water. Some climbed the steep canyon walls and held on to trees and cracks in the rock.

Most, however, could not escape. *"I'm stuck,"* State Trooper Willis H. Purdy radioed to headquarters, *"I'm right in the middle of it, I can't get out."* Seconds later, the flood swept him away. Sergeant Purdy's body was found 8 miles (13 km) down the canyon.

In just two hours, the Big Thompson Canyon flash flood killed 145 people. The flood destroyed about 600 houses and businesses and damaged hundreds more. Fixing the damage cost more than $40 million.

Flood Country

FLOODS CAN HAPPEN ALMOST ANYWHERE. FLOODS STRIKE MORE PLACES THAN ANY OTHER DISASTER EXCEPT FIRES. THEY OCCUR EVEN IN DRY DESERTS.

In the United States, almost 20 million homes, businesses, schools, and other buildings are in areas with a high risk of floods. Some are near the Atlantic Ocean or the Gulf of Mexico. Others are near rivers and streams. In the rest of the world, about one billion people live in flood country. Some of the world's worst floods have occurred in China, Bangladesh, and India.

SEACOASTS AND RIVERS

Hurricanes and other storms cause flood disasters along seacoasts. These storms often drop heavy rain that makes lakes, rivers, and streams overflow their banks. A hurricane's strong winds also can push seawater onto the land.

As storms move inland, the rain can cause flooding far away from the coast. In 2004 Hurricanes Ivan and Frances caused floods in Pennsylvania, West

FLOOD CITY

Venice, Italy, floods more often than almost any city in the world. Venice is built on islands connected by bridges. The city is close to sea level, and it is slowly sinking. The ocean's surface rises and falls each day. When it rises, ocean water covers Venice's streets.

Most of the city's floods amount to only a few inches of water. But they happen often. In some years, Venice has more than one flood a week.

Two girls wade past a shop in Venice, Italy, in floodwater that is almost knee deep.

FLOOD COUNTRY

The Netherlands (also known as Holland) is on the North Sea, where storms often send huge waves crashing over the shore. About one-third of the country is below sea level (the height of the ocean's surface). The land would fill up like a bowl if water got in. Much of the rest is barely 1 yard (1 m) above sea level. Even a small storm surge would rush over the countryside.

One great flood in the Netherlands in 1953 killed 1,800 people and left 300,000 people homeless. Afterward, the government decided to stop the floods once and for all. It built a system of dikes (walls), dams, and other barriers. The American Society of Civil Engineers lists this flood control system as one of the Seven Wonders of the Modern World.

More than 1,000 people were killed by flooding in the Netherlands in February 1953. This photo shows the island of Schouwen, which was covered by water.

Virginia, and Ohio. The disasters damaged thousands of buildings.

Some of the worst floods in the United States have occurred along the Mississippi River and rivers that flow into it. These rivers naturally overflow their banks every few years.

OTHER DANGER ZONES

Places that get cloudbursts (short, heavy rainstorms) also may become flash flood disaster zones. The Big Thompson Canyon flash flood killed 145 people.

Strong winds blowing across lakes can make the lakeshores a disaster zone. The winds can push water from one end of the lake to the other. The extra water may overflow and flood nearby areas.

Floods also can occur in areas where large amounts of water are stored. These include dams, reservoirs, and storage tanks. If the water breaks out, it will flood nearby buildings.

DISASTER ZONES

Floods happen all around the world. This map shows just a few of the major flood disasters that have taken place over the centuries. Death tolls are given for the deadliest floods.

The Netherlands
1228 (100,000 deaths)
1287 (50,000 deaths)
1421 (100,000 deaths)
1634 (15,000 deaths)

NEVA RIVER,
Saint Petersburg, Russia 1824

YELLOW RIVER, China
1642 (300,000+ deaths)
1887 (900,000+ deaths)
1938 (500,000+ deaths)

Shalan Township,
China 2005

Central Europe 2002
Florence, Italy 1333

YANGTZE RIVER, China
1911 (100,000+ deaths)
1931 (3,700,000 deaths)
1998 (3,000 deaths)

ARNO RIVER, Italy 1966

EUROPE

ASIA

Tehran, Iran 1954

TAGUS RIVER
Lisbon, Portugal 1755

AFRICA

South Asia 2004
(155,000 deaths)

Nile River, Sudan 1988

Haiphong, Vietnam
1881 (300,000 deaths)

Mumbai, India
1876
(100,000 deaths)

Coringa, India
1839 (300,000+ deaths)

Southeastern Africa 2000

AUSTRALIA

Bengal, India
1876 (100,000 deaths)

Bangladesh
1970 (500,000+ deaths)
1974 (25,000+ deaths)
1991 (131,000 deaths)

NORTH AMERICA

Great Midwest Flood
1993

BIG THOMPSON RIVER, Colorado 1976

New England 2006

New Orleans, Louisiana 2005

Johnstown, PA U.S.A.
1889 (2,200 deaths)

Galveston, TX U.S.A
1900 (8,000+ deaths)

Haiti
2004 (3,000+ deaths)

SOUTH AMERICA

The *snakes,*" said Virgie Sadler, who had watched them slithering through the flood near her home in Cape Girardeau, Missouri. *"That's what I hated most of all. Snakes and slugs and the smell of rotten fish. The odor is unbelievable."* Sadler was talking about one of the greatest flood disasters in U.S. history.

The trouble started in 1992, with a wet autumn in the central United States. Heavy snow fell during the winter and melted in the spring. By April 1993, the ground was like a wet sponge. It could not soak up another drop of water.

Everyone hoped for dry weather. Instead, they got more rain. *"I think everybody was ready for some . . . serious flooding,"* said Kenneth D. King, a flood expert at the National Weather Service, *"but nobody thought it would last all summer."*

Rain fell in buckets! In June and

July, there were 12 storms with rainfalls of 6 to 12 inches (15 to 30 cm). Water overflowed the banks of the Mississippi River, the Missouri River, and hundreds of small rivers and streams. The flood lasted until October.

"The water was so high, you might only see the tops of grain silos [storage towers] . . . and . . . the roof of one of the taller buildings," said Bob Brakenridge, a scientist who studies floods. *"Even from up in the air, you could look out almost to the horizon and there was nothing but water."*

"Just the sheer magnitude [size] was incredible," said Tom Harris, a U.S. Geological Survey scientist who studies floods. *"At Waverly [Missouri], the Missouri River was basically 10 miles [1.6 km] wide, normally when you see it, it's 800 to 900 feet [240 to 270 m] wide."*

The water was up to 20 feet (6 m) deep. It covered parts of nine states: North Dakota, South Dakota, Nebraska,

Flooding of the Mississippi River ruined this corn crop in Illinois.

Kansas, Minnesota, Iowa, Missouri, Wisconsin, and Illinois. About 75 towns were completely underwater.

Tens of thousands of people had to evacuate. Many never returned because the floods totally destroyed 10,000 homes. The floodwater caused $15 billion in damage.

> **It just became like a monster that you couldn't catch up to. And it just kept coming!**
> —Dave Mueller, U.S. Army flood expert, describing efforts to control flooding in the Midwest in 1993

Measuring Floods

THE ANCIENT EGYPTIANS WERE THE FIRST PEOPLE TO MEASURE FLOODS. ALMOST 3,800 YEARS AGO, THEY INVENTED THE NILEOMETER, A DEVICE TO MEASURE THE FLOODING OF THE NILE RIVER. A NILEOMETER WAS LIKE A LONG RULER PLACED IN THE RIVER. IT HAD LINES THAT SHOWED THE WATER'S DEPTH.

People wanted the Nile to flood in those days. Each year it overflowed and left a layer of silt on its floodplain. This rich soil helped farmers grow more crops.

The amount of silt determined how much food could be grown. If the flood was big enough, there would be plenty of food. If it was too small, crops would fail and people would starve.

EYES IN THE SKY

In modern times, scientists use electronic devices to keep an eye on rivers and streams. They have placed hundreds of these devices in rivers and streams that often flood. The devices measure the amount of water flowing past them. They radio the measurements to satellites (unmanned spacecraft) orbiting Earth. The satellites send the information to computers back on the ground. Scientists use it to issue flood warnings and to measure the size of floods.

FAST FACT

The Yellow River runs for 3,400 miles (5,500 km) through northern China. It has killed more people than any other feature of Earth's surface. More than 6 million people have died in Yellow River floods since 1887.

This man is standing beside a nileometer in Cairo, Egypt. The markings were used by the ancient Egyptians to measure the Nile River's summer floods.

Scientists also use images (pictures) taken by satellites to measure the size of floods. These images show exactly where flood damage is happening. This information helps relief organizations (groups that help people affected by disasters) decide where to send help.

THE 100-YEAR FLOOD

Scientists have developed scales to measure other kinds of disasters. The Richter scale, for instance, measures the strength of earthquakes. However, there is no scale for measuring a flood's impact.

The damage a flood causes depends on the depth of the water, how fast it flows, and how long it stays on the land. Deep water that flows fast causes more damage than shallow, slow water.

An inflatable rubber dam stretches across the Tankabati River in Kalauzan, Bangladesh.

BALLOONS THAT STOP FLOODS

Levees stop floods by keeping water from spilling over riverbanks. But people living behind levees can't enjoy a view of the river. Inflatable levees are one solution to this problem.

Inflatable levees are big rubber bags attached to the riverbank. People can see right over the bags when the water is at its normal level. When the river rises, however, a machine automatically inflates (blows up) the bags. They rise up to form a wall that keeps water in the river. When the flood threat has passed, the levee deflates again.

These flood stoppers are used on the Susquehanna River in Pennsylvania, the Los Angeles River in California, and a few other places in the United States. Japan has hundreds of them.

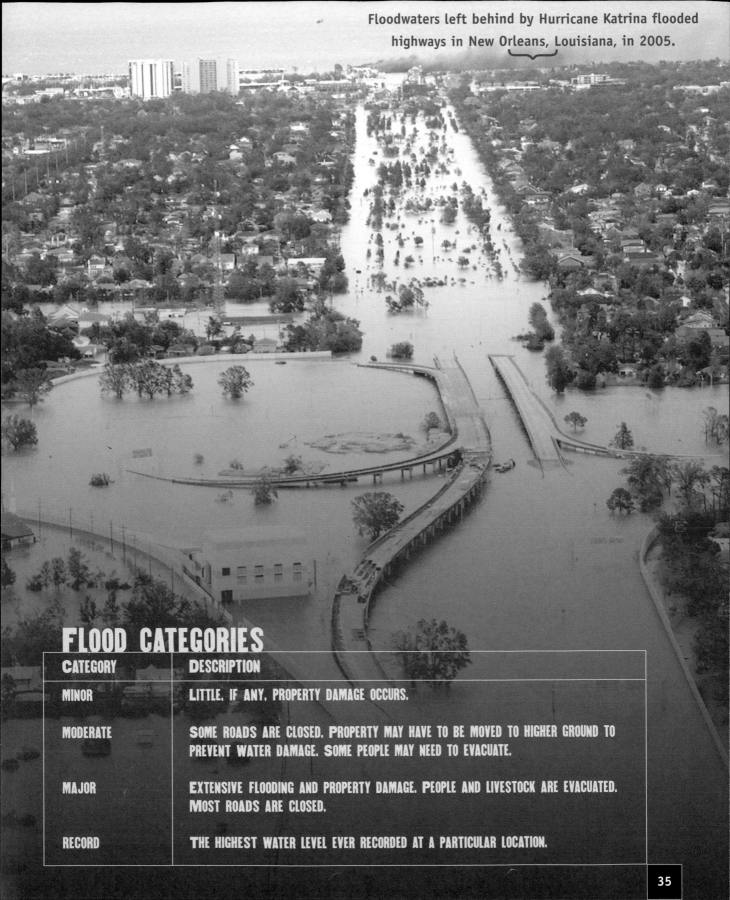

Floodwaters left behind by Hurricane Katrina flooded highways in New Orleans, Louisiana, in 2005.

FLOOD CATEGORIES

CATEGORY	DESCRIPTION
MINOR	LITTLE, IF ANY, PROPERTY DAMAGE OCCURS.
MODERATE	SOME ROADS ARE CLOSED. PROPERTY MAY HAVE TO BE MOVED TO HIGHER GROUND TO PREVENT WATER DAMAGE. SOME PEOPLE MAY NEED TO EVACUATE.
MAJOR	EXTENSIVE FLOODING AND PROPERTY DAMAGE. PEOPLE AND LIVESTOCK ARE EVACUATED. MOST ROADS ARE CLOSED.
RECORD	THE HIGHEST WATER LEVEL EVER RECORDED AT A PARTICULAR LOCATION.

Floods that last a long time cause more damage to crops, roads, and buildings. A flood's location also counts. Floods in cities cause more damage than those in the country.

Scientists may decide that a certain flood is a "50-year flood" or a "100-year flood." That doesn't mean that the flood *lasts* for 50 or 100 years. It means a flood that bad happens only once every 50 years or 100 years.

DID YOU KNOW?

Dams hold back water from heavy rainfalls. The water stays in a big lake behind the dam, rather than flooding the land. Most dams have a section called a spillway. The spillway lets some of the water flow through. In some dams, the moving water powers generators—machines that make electricity.

In 2006 the Chinese government finished building a dam across the Yangtze River. The Three Gorges Dam is the biggest in the world. It will prevent floods and produce electricity for the people of China.

If a dam breaks, however, it can cause a terrible flood. The great Johnstown, Pennsylvania, flood happened in 1889 because an old dam broke.

The Three Gorges Dam across the Yangtze River in China is the largest water control project in the world.

In early 2000, storms brought heavy rains to southern Africa. Flooding in central Mozambique stranded about 100,000 people in trees and on rooftops.

2005 GREAT FLOODS IN CHINA

Residents use boats to travel down a flooded street in Wuzhou, China. In some areas, the flooding reached the third floor of buildings.

Guoqin Zhao rushed to her granddaughters' school on June 10, 2005. More than 380 children and teachers were in the school. It was near a river, in the town of Shalan in the northeastern part of China. *"Teacher!"* Zhao shouted. *"Please stop the class. The dam upstream is broken!"*

People living in villages farther up the river had called friends in Shalan. Their telephone calls warned that the river had become a killer. Heavy rains had made the river wider and deeper than usual. The water was rushing down toward Shalan. When the water reached Shalan, it would flood the land.

Unfortunately, the teacher ignored Zhao. She kept the pupils in class. Zhao grabbed her granddaughters and took them home. Two hours later, the floodwater smashed into the school. It killed at least 99 students.

Parents heard about the flood.

They raced to the school. When Jia Yibo arrived at the school, he found 40 bodies floating in the waist-deep, dirty water. One was Jia's son. *"My son was placed on a desk and the desk's surface was only a little higher than the water level,"* Jia said. *"His nose, ears and mouth were filled with mud . . . and when I touched him, I found he was dead."*

When we forced our way in, there were bodies floating everywhere. The parents went mad. Everybody was crying.

—Sun Xiuqin, describing attempts to rescue children from a flooded school in Shalan, China, in 2005

The flood at the Shalan school was only one small part of a bigger disaster. Heavy rain caused floods all over northeastern and central China. Some of the worst damage happened when the Pearl River overflowed its banks near Hong Kong.

"Yesterday was the worst flooding I have seen in my eight years in Hong Kong," said Devon Bovenlander. *"It was terrible. Whole streets were turned into rivers."* The rushing water knocked down bridges and ripped up roads. *"Some roads flowed like a rapid river,"* said Nicholas Lee.

The floods killed at least 536 people. About 1.5 million people had to be evacuated. Tens of thousands of houses and other buildings were destroyed.

People suffered long after the water drained away. Families had to live in shelters or with relatives until their houses could be rebuilt. The flood destroyed rice and other crops growing on 1.6 million acres (650,000 hectares) of farmland. There were shortages of food, so people had to pay higher prices for it. The damage cost at least $2.5 billion.

As the floodwaters recede in Wuzhou, China, garbage piles up in the streets *(left)*. A Xinshao County resident rests in her flood-stricken village *(above)*.

People Helping People

STRANGE AS IT MAY SOUND, ONE OF THE FIRST THINGS THAT FLOOD VICTIMS NEED AFTER THE FLOODWATER GOES AWAY IS MORE WATER. THEY NEED CLEAN WATER TO DRINK. WITHOUT SAFE DRINKING WATER, FOOD, AND MEDICINE, PEOPLE WHO SURVIVE FLOODS ARE IN DANGER EVEN AFTER THE IMMEDIATE DISASTER ENDS. IF THE FLOOD DESTROYED HOMES, SURVIVORS ALSO NEED A PLACE TO LIVE.

Flood survivors may get sick from drinking dirty floodwater or from not having enough food to eat. Germs in the water can infect cuts and scrapes. Other injuries suffered during the flood may also need a doctor's attention.

In some great floods, four times as many people die afterward as in the high water. Preventing more deaths is the first job for relief workers. Then relief workers can help victims get their lives back to normal.

A DRINK OF CLEAN WATER

After the great 2005 floods in India, almost 500,000 survivors did not have clean drinking water, food, shelter, or medicine. These people had been evacuated from the flooded areas. They were living in outdoor camps, schools, and other buildings.

DISASTER RELIEF MYTH

People who want to help flood victims often think of collecting and sending blankets, used clothing, and shoes. However, that may not be the best way to help. It often costs more to sort, pack, and ship the donations than it would to buy new items. Donating money to a relief organization may be the best way to help. These donations enable relief organizations to buy exactly what victims need most.

In 1994, following Tropical Storm Alberto, the Flint River flooded much of Albany, Georgia.

Countries around the world joined together in a relief effort. Governments, churches, the Indian Red Cross, and private disaster relief groups provided millions of dollars in help. These organizations rushed in hundreds of thousands of bottles of water. They also supplied bottles of a chemical that kills germs in water, making it pure enough to drink. Airplanes and trucks brought in tons of food. Hundreds of doctors and nurses and tons of medicine arrived from parts of India that had not been flooded and from other parts of the world.

RELIEF PROBLEMS

Safe water, food, and medicine must arrive in a disaster area quickly. Getting it there within the first day or two after a flood can be very difficult. Flooding often destroys or blocks airport runways and roads. Relief planes cannot land. Trucks and cars cannot reach victims, especially those in remote areas. "All roads and trains were blocked, which made delivering relief supplies difficult," Darryl D'Monte said about the relief work in India.

RELIEF ARRIVES

With their homes destroyed, millions of people needed shelter after the flooding in India. Relief organizations gave out thousands of big sheets of plastic. Flood victims stretched the plastic sheets over boards and sticks to build huts and tents.

Many victims lived together in camps. Having many survivors in one place made it easier for relief organizations to provide them with water, food, and medicine. Some camps held hundreds of men, women, and children.

This camp in Huayin, China, is a temporary home for flood victims.

Rescue workers bring food and bottled water to flood victims in Mumbai, India, in 2005.

> " *Conditions* are *getting worse* every day. *The water is rising* and bringing in *more filth.* We are living in an open sewer. "
> —Abu Kalam, who was in a flood that covered most of Bangladesh in 2004

Workers passed out relief kits. These packages contained blankets, clothing, pots and pans for cooking, matches, and candles for light. People also got packages of food.

Flood victims had to stay in the camps until new homes could be built. Rebuilding may take months. In some horrible floods, such as the 2005 Hurricane Katrina disaster, some homes may never be rebuilt. People just move away and live in other areas.

RECOVERY AND REBUILDING

Disaster victims usually need money. It costs a lot to rebuild homes, buy new furniture and clothing, and get life back to normal. In the United States, flood victims often get help. Many people who live in flood zones buy insurance from the Federal Emergency Management Agency (FEMA). FEMA is the U.S. government agency that prepares for disasters and organizes recovery efforts. FEMA lends people money to help fix or rebuild damaged homes and other buildings. FEMA and other government agencies also provide individuals, businesses, and cities with other help.

FAST FACT

The American Red Cross is one of the largest disaster relief organizations in the United States. The famous nurse Clara Barton founded it in 1881. The Johnstown Flood was the Red Cross's first major disaster relief effort. Clara Barton led the relief team. Red Cross workers provided victims of the flood with a place to live, food, and other aid.

In other countries, however, people often have no flood insurance. If the government is poor, it may be unable to help. People may never fully recover from the disaster. Disasters may make the entire country poorer. Then the next disaster will be even more difficult.

This house in Weesenstein, Germany, was
destroyed by floodwater in August 2002.

2005
FLOODING OF NEW ORLEANS

Emergency workers in New Orleans, Louisiana, rescue people who were stranded in their homes.

Everyone knew that the city of New Orleans was in great danger from flooding. Much of New Orleans is built on land shaped like a soup bowl. Water from ordinary rainfall collects in the bowl. It has to be pumped out. Also, the city is surrounded by bodies of water—the Mississippi River, Lake Pontchartrain, and Lake Borgne. Nearby is the Gulf of Mexico.

People built levees to hold back the river and lake water. They installed powerful pumps to remove rainwater. People made jokes about New Orleans filling up with water. But few of them believed that it would really happen.

Disaster finally struck in August 2005. Hurricane Katrina roared toward the coast of the Gulf of Mexico with winds of 140 miles (230 km) per hour. Katrina's fierce winds pushed a huge wall of water toward New Orleans. This storm surge was up to 30 feet (9 m) high and 200 miles (320 km) long.

The levees protecting New Orleans could not hold back the water. They broke, and water poured into the city. **"Within 15 minutes you had 6 feet [2 m]** *of water in your home. . . ."* said J. Michael Brown. *"In about 30 minutes I had 12 feet [4 m]. Across the street there was probably 15 feet [5 m] of water.... As far as you could see, there was nothing but black water."*

At least 80 percent of New Orleans was flooded. The water was 20 feet (6 m) deep in some places. Police told everyone to evacuate the city before Katrina arrived. Some, however, couldn't get out. Almost 40,000 people were stranded for days before help arrived. They had to live in horrible conditions. There was no electricity or air-conditioning in 90°F (32°C) weather. Toilets overflowed because there was no running water. People could not shower. Food ran out, and no medical help was available.

Adele Bertucci spent four days on the roof of her home waiting to be rescued. *"Every boat that passed by was filled with people—people and dogs, people in wheelchairs,"* she said. Finally, a helicopter lowered a special chair connected to a rope and lifted Bertucci off the roof.

Everyone in Sidney Smith's home had to go upstairs to escape the floodwater. The water was filthy and dangerous to touch. *"The area had become truly toxic,"* Smith said.

The disaster was one of the worst in U.S. history. At least 1,200 people died. Hundreds of others were injured. There was at least $150 billion in damage. Many of the people whose homes were destroyed moved away and never returned to New Orleans.

"We had heard about corpses floating down the street. There were dead animals in the water.... There was gasoline. There was urine. There was feces [solid body wastes]."

—Sidney Smith, describing conditions experienced by survivors of Hurricane Katrina in New Orleans

47

The Future

PAST FLOODS HAVE TAUGHT IMPORTANT LESSONS. THESE DISASTERS HAVE HELPED PEOPLE UNDERSTAND THE IMPORTANCE OF PREVENTING FLOODS. PEOPLE ALSO HAVE LEARNED THAT ADVANCE WARNING SYSTEMS CAN SAVE LIVES IN A FLOOD.

After a disastrous flood along the Mississippi River in 1927, the U.S. government began a huge flood control project. It involved building more than 1,500 miles (2,400 km) of levees to keep the river from overflowing. The project also included the construction of dams, canals, and other structures. Without this flood control system, the 1993 floods would have been much worse.

People also learned from the Big Thompson River flood in 1976. It led the National Weather Service to set up early warning systems in places at risk for flash floods. These systems use sensors that keep track of how rapidly rain is falling in an area. The sensors radio that information to a central station, which issues a warning when a flash flood may happen.

Many huge floods along the Yellow River taught the Chinese government that their country needed flood control projects. In 2000 China completed a huge dam that already has prevented some floods.

LESSONS NOT LEARNED

Since 1993 billions of dollars' worth of homes, shopping centers, offices, and schools have been built on land that was underwater during the Great Midwest Flood. People are planning to construct many more buildings on other floodplains. Once the water goes away, it is easy to forget the danger. But when we don't learn from the past, history may repeat itself.

Some of the homes in this neighborhood in East Grand Forks, Minnesota, floated off their foundations when the Red River flooded in 1997.

The dam holds back water and releases it a little at a time. China plans to build nearly 30 more dams to tame the Yellow River.

MOVING OUT OF HARM'S WAY

Flood control projects are only one way to prevent future flood disasters. People must also be kept from building homes and other structures in areas where floods often occur. FEMA has prepared maps of areas where flooding is certain to occur in the future. Cities use the maps to make rules that keep people from building homes on floodplains.

After floods, FEMA sometimes buys damaged homes that are on floodplains. The people who owned the homes use the money they receive to buy new houses in safer places. Their old homes are torn down.

"When you get the people out of the floodplain, you don't have to boat in and rescue residents," said Jan Horton, a flood control official for the State of Illinois. "You don't have to evacuate, put up road blocks, and rebuild where the floodwaters will surely be back."

A weather forecaster issues a flood warning over the radio.

ON THE WATCH FOR FLOODS

Children and adults should learn about flood hazards no matter where they live. It is especially important if you live in an area where floods often occur.

Make sure you understand the terms used to describe floods. The government issues a flood watch when flooding is possible within 12 to 24 hours. During a flood watch, stay tuned to the news for more information. A flood warning is announced when floods are already occurring or will occur soon. If you are told to evacuate, do so immediately.

A woman rides a floating bed outside her flooded house in Sultan Kudarat, Philippines, in 2004.

People usually are very happy to be living in a safer place. "We don't worry about floods in Arnold anymore," said Joe Moore, of Arnold, Missouri. "It used to be every time it rained hard, we flooded. But not anymore."

FEAR-FREE FLOODS

Floods can cause terrible disasters. They have killed and injured thousands of people in the past. But don't let worries about floods spoil the fun of watching the rain or a flowing river.

Flood disasters are quite rare. You probably will never even see a flood. And if flooding does happen where you live, following a few safety tips (on page 53) can reduce your chances of being hurt.

A 2005 flood of the Emme River washed away much of a main street in Werthenstein, Switzerland.

FLOOD SAFETY TIPS

- Do not walk through moving floodwater. Just 6 inches (15 cm) of moving water can knock you down. You could be swept away and drown. If you must walk in a flood, walk where the water is not moving. Use a stick to check the firmness of the ground in front of you.

- Warn your parents not to drive through floodwater. It may be deeper than anyone thinks. Just 2 feet (0.6 m) of flowing water can sweep away a car or even a big SUV.

- Prepare a disaster supply kit with your family. Include enough food and water for each person for at least three days. Check the list of items to include at www.disastereducation.org/guide and www.fema.gov/rrr/talkdiz/kit.shtm#water.

- Families should agree on a place to meet after the disaster, in case they get separated.

- Return home only when emergency officials say it is okay. Be very careful when entering a flood-damaged building. There may be hidden damage. Parts of the building may cave in without warning.

- Don't swim or play in floodwater. Don't get it in your mouth. It is filthy and loaded with germs.

- Wash your hands often with soap and clean water if you touch floodwater.

- Throw away food that has come in contact with floodwaters.

- Listen to news reports to find out if it is safe to drink water from the faucets. News reports also will say where you can get help to find clothing, food, medical care, and a place to stay.

Timeline

1099 High tides and storm waves flood the coast of England causing 100,000 people to drown.

1421 Dikes in Holland break, drowning 100,000 people.

1755 An earthquake in Lisbon, Portugal, causes a tsunami that kills people who had sought safety on the banks of the Tagus River.

1824 The Neva River in Saint Petersburg, Russia, floods after an ice jam blocks the river.

1839 A 40-foot (10 m) tsunami wipes out the city of Coringa, India.

1876 A cyclone near the Megha River in Bengal, India, drowns 100,000 people. Another 100,000 die from starvation and disease.

1883 The Krakatau volcano in Indonesia erupts, causing a tsunami that carries ships more than 1 mile (1.6 km) inland.

1887 The Yellow River in China floods more than 50,000 square miles (130,000 sq. km) and claims at least 900,000 lives.

1889 The South Fork Dam, outside Johnstown, Pennsylvania, bursts, causing a flash flood that destroys the city.

1900 A hurricane and flooding in Galveston, Texas, claim more than 8,000 lives.

1911 The Yangtze River in China overflows, killing 100,000 people.

1919 A storage tank with 2.3 million gallons (8.7 million l) of molasses explodes and sends a 15-foot-high (4.6 m) wall of molasses through parts of the city of Boston, Massachusetts.

1931 An estimated 3.7 million people die when the Yangtze River in China floods again.

1938 Chiang Kai-shek orders Chinese citizens to destroy dikes to prevent the Japanese from advancing into China *(left)*. At least half a million people die from the flooding.

1953 The North Sea flows over dikes in 100 different spots in the Netherlands, flooding 4 million acres (1.6 million hectares).

1954 A flash flood in Tehran, Iran, overwhelms 2,000 people who had gathered for a religious service.

1964 An Alaskan earthquake produces tsunami waves 35 feet (11 m) high.

1970 Egypt's Aswan Dam is completed.

1974 A flood in Bangladesh kills about 1,200 people. Another 24,500 die from starvation and disease that follows the flood *(left)*.

1976 The Big Thompson Canyon, Colorado, flash flood kills 145 people.

1988 Unusually heavy rains cause the Nile River to flood in Sudan, leaving 1.5 million people homeless.

1991 Flooding from a cyclone in Bangladesh kills approximately 131,000 people and leaves 9 million people homeless.

1993 The Great Midwest Flood in the United States hits nine states, lasts more than four months, and results in at least $15 billion in damages.

1998 Cutting down forests in China causes floods resulting in 3,000 deaths and $20 billion in damages.

2000 Hurricane Eline brings heavy rain to southeastern Africa and leaves 500,000 people homeless.

2002 The Great European Flood starts in the Czech Republic and spreads across central Europe.

2004 Hurricanes Ivan and Frances cause flooding in Pennsylvania, Ohio, and West Virginia.

Hurricane Jeanne kills more than 3,000 people and leaves at least 200,000 homeless in Haiti.

A tsunami caused by an earthquake in the Indian Ocean inundates South Asia and kills more than 155,000 people.

2005 Floods kill at least 536 people in Shalan Township in northeastern China.

Heavy rains cause massive flooding in Mumbai, India.

Hurricane Katrina floods the Gulf Coast of the United States.

2006 Heavy rains cause massive flooding in the northeastern United States *(right)*.

Glossary

cloudburst: a short, heavy rainstorm

dam: a wall built across a river to hold back some or all of the water

dike: a bank built along a river or seashore to prevent flooding

evacuate: to move to a safe place until an emergency is over

flash flood: a flood that happens with little warning. Heavy rainfall causes most flash floods.

floodplain: land along the sides of a river that is covered by water when the river floods

flood warning: a notice given by the government when floods are already occurring or will occur soon

flood watch: a notice given by the government when flooding is possible within 12 to 24 hours

levee: a raised bank of earth built along a river to prevent flooding

reservoir: a lake that forms behind a dam

sandbag: a cloth or plastic bag filled with sand that is used to make walls to protect buildings from flooding

sea level: the height of the ocean's surface

silt: fine particles of soil that can be picked up by flowing water

storm surge: a wall of water that is pushed along by a hurricane

tsunami: a large ocean wave caused by shock waves from an earthquake, a volcano, or an underwater landslide

Places to Visit

Delta Cultural Center
http://www.arkansasstateparks.com/media/
display.asp?id=119
Visit the Delta Cultural Center in Helena,
Arkansas, and see displays about the Mississippi
River.

Johnstown Flood Museum
http://www.artcom.com/Museums/nv/gl/15901.htm
Find out all about the flooding of Johnstown,
Pennsylvania, in 1889.

Museum in the Park at Chief Logan State Park
http://www.wvculture.org/agency/press/
loganbuffck.html
The Museum in the Park at Chief Logan State Park
in West Virginia has an exhibition on the Buffalo
Creek flood that devastated the area in 1972.

Teton Flood Museum
http://www.rexcc.com/thingstodo/attractions/
tetonflood.html
See signs of the devastating flooding from the
collapse of the Great Teton Dam in 1976. During
this flood, about 80 billion gallons (300 billion l) of
floodwater came roaring down on Rexburg, Idaho.

Source Notes

4 Hafeez Irani, quoted in "India Floods Toll Reaches
   1,000," *CNN.com*, August 1, 2005,
   http://www.cnn.com/2005/WORLD/asiapcf/
   08/01/india.flood/index.html (August 14, 2006).

4 Sikander Zhaid, quoted in "India Counts the
   Cost of Floods," *BBC News*, August 2, 2005,
   http://news.bbc.co.uk/go/pr/fr/-/1/hi/
   world/south_asia/4737187.stm (June 6, 2006).

5 Anjali Krishnan, "Wading All Night through
   Mumbai," *BBC News*, July 28, 2005,
   http://news.bbc.co.uk/1/hi/world/south_asia/
   4724245.stm (June 6, 2006).

8 Bob Gieseke, quoted in Bill Graham, "Relief
   Workers, Families Recall Devastation of 1993,"
   Kansas City Star, July 10, 2003.

10 Bev Anderson, quoted in "The 1993 Great
    Midwest Flood: Voices 10 Years Later" (Jessup,
    MD: Federal Emergency Management Agency,
    2003), 32.

11 Yetta Chin, quoted in Katie Zezima, "New
    England Floods Force Thousands from
    Homes," *New York Times*, May 15, 2006.

12–13 M. Elizabeth Morgan, quoted in "The Johnstown
    Flood," *The Johnstown Flood 1889*, April 16, 1995,
    http://ourworld.compuserve.com/homepages/
    Glsenberg/flood.htm (June 7, 2006).

13 C. W. Linthicum, quoted in Willis Fletcher
    Johnson, "Chapter 5," *History of the Johnstown
    Flood*, October 14, 1999, http://prr.railfan.net/
    documents/JohnstownFlood/chapter5.html (June
    10, 2006).

13 Charles Pitcarin, quoted in Willis Fletcher Johnson, "Chapter 5," *History of the Johnstown Flood*, October 14, 1999, http://prr.railfan.net/documents/JohnstownFlood/chapter5.html (June 10, 2006).

13 Anna Fenn, quoted in "Survivor Stories of the Johnstown Flood," *Johnstown Flood Museum*, n.d., http://www.jaha.org/FloodMuseum/survivors.html (June 11, 2006).

17 Lucy Chapman, quoted in Dick Meadows, "Horror of the Floods Undimmed," *BBC News*, January 23, 2003, http://news.bbc.co.uk/1/hi/england/2678105.stm (June 11, 2006).

18 Alcutt McNaghten, "The Flood as Experienced by Alcutt McNaghten," *Flood Survivors*, December 2, 2002, http://folsommuseum.netfirms.com/flood_survivors.htm (June 7, 2006).

20 Danny Shahaf, quoted in "Survivors Tell of Tsunami Train Horror," *BBC News*, December 30, 2004, http://news.bbc.co.uk/1/hi/world/south_asia/4132247.stm (August 15, 2006).

24–25 Lisa Wycoff, "Eyewitness Stories," *Super70s.com*, April 16, 2006, http://super70s.com/Community/forums/2313/ShowThread.aspx (June 10, 2006).

25 Robert Watson, interviewed by Charlene Tresner, "Big Thompson Flood," *Larimer County Water Ways Oral Histories*, September 9, 1976, http://history.fcgov.com/archive/lcdi/oralhistories.htm (June 7, 2006).

25 State Trooper Willis H. Purdy, quoted in "About CSP: In Memoriam," *Colorado State Patrol*, October 14, 2004, http://www.csp.state.co.us/memorium.cfm (June 8, 2006).

30 Virgie Sadler, quoted in *The 1993 Great Midwest Flood: Voices 10 Years Later* (Jessup, MD: Federal Emergency Management Agency, May 2003), 41.

30 Kenneth D. King, quoted in "Quiet Beginning Heralded Nation's Worst Flood in 1993," *NOAA News Online*, April 2, 2003, http://www.noaanews.noaa.gov/stories/s1125.htm (June 9, 2006).

30–31 Bob Brakenridge, quoted in "Charting the Waters," *Dartmouth Faculty Scholarship Today*, 2003, http://www.dartmouth.edu/~dartfac/features/waters.html (June 9, 2006).

31 Tom Harris, quoted in Bill Graham, "Relief Workers, Families Recall Devastation of 1993," *Kansas City Star*, July 10, 2003.

31 Dave Mueller, quoted in "Flood!" *NOVA*, May 6, 1997, http://www.pbs.org/wgbh/nova/transcripts/2307tfloo.html (June 9, 2006).

38 Guoqin Zhao, quoted in "The Flash Flood Swept Through Shalan Town Elementary School," *China Digital Times*, June 16, 2005, http://chinadigitaltimes.net/2005/06/xiaorong_the_fl_1.php (August 15, 2006).

38–39 Jia Yibo, quoted in "Chinese School Flood Kills Scores, " *BBC News*, June 13, 2005, http://news.bbc.co.uk/2/hi/asia-pacific/4086602.stm (June 7, 2006).

39 Sun Xiuqin, quoted in Ching-Ching Ni, "Parents Mourn Loss of Children in Flash Flood," *Los Angeles Times*, June 14, 2005.

39 Devon Bovenlander, quoted in "China Flood Death Toll 'Over 500'," *BBC News*, June 25, 2005, http://news.bbc.co.uk/2/hi/asia-pacific/4617891.stm (June 7, 2006).

39 Nicholas Lee, quoted in ""China Flood Death Toll 'Over 500'," *BBC News*.

42 Darryl D'Monte, "A Spate of Neighborliness," *India Together* (Mumbai, India), March 28, 2006.

43 Abu Kalam, quoted in "Bangladesh Flood Crisis Worsens," *BBC News,* July 24, 2004, http://news.bbc.co.uk/go/pr/fr/-/1/hi/world/south_asia/3928463.stm (June 7, 2006).

46–47 J. Michael Brown, interviewed by Shannon Gibney, "New Orleans: Survivor Stories," *City Pages,* September 20, 2005, http://citypages.com/databank/26/1294/article13694.asp?page=3 (June 10, 2006).

47 Adele Bertucci, interviewed by Mike Mosedale, "New Orleans: Survivor Stories," *City Pages,* September 20, 2005, http://citypages.com/databank/26/1294/article13694.asp?page=2 (June 10, 2006).

47 Sidney Smith, interviewed by Mike Mosedale, "New Orleans: Survivor Stories," *City Pages,* September 20, 2005, http://citypages.com/databank/26/1294/article13694.asp?page=18 (June 10, 2006).

47 Ibid.

50 Jan Horton, quoted in "The 1993 Great Midwest Flood: Voices 10 Years Later," *FEMA.gov,* May 2003, http://www.fema.gov/pdf/nfip/voices_anthology1.pdf (June 7, 2006).

52 Joe Moore, quoted in "The 1993 Great Midwest Flood: Voices 10 Years Later," *FEMA.gov.*

Selected Bibliography

Allaby, Michael. *A Chronology of Weather: Dangerous Weather.* New York: Facts on File, 1998.

———. *Floods.* New York: Facts on File, 1998.

Barry, John M. *Rising Tide: The Great Flood of 1927 and How It Changed America.* New York: Simon & Schuster, 1997.

Collier, Michael. *Floods, Droughts, and Climate Change.* Tucson: University of Arizona Press, 2002.-

Davis, Lee Allyn. *Natural Disasters.* New York: Facts on File, 2002.

Fagan, Brian M. *Floods, Famines and Emperors: El Niño and the Fate of Civilizations.* New York: Basic Books, 1999.

Gallagher, Jim. *The Johnstown Flood.* Philadelphia: Chelsea House Publishers, 2000.

Gorman, Jeff. *Atlas of Natural Disasters.* New York: Michael Friedman Publishing Group, 2002.

Miller, E. Willard. *Natural Disasters: Floods: A Reference Handbook.* Santa Barbara, CA: ABC-CLIO, 2000.

Vogel, Carole Garbuny. *Nature's Fury: Eyewitness Reports of Natural Disaster.* New York: Scholastic, 2000.

Wright, Ted. *Wright's Complete Disaster Survival Manual.* Norfolk, VA: Hampton Roads Publishing Company, 1993.

Further Resources

BOOKS

Calhoun, Mary. *Flood*. New York: Morrow Junior Books, 1997. This is the fictional story of Sarajean and her family, who were determined to remain on their farm when the Mississippi River flooded in 1993.

Duey, Kathleen, and Karen A. Bale. *Flood: Mississippi 1927*. New York: Aladdin, 1998. In this novel, Molly and Garrett are saving their money to escape from rural Mississippi when a flood threatens to wash their money away.

Goodman, Susan E. *Animal Rescue: The Best Job There Is*. New York: Simon & Schuster, 2000. Follow John Walsh, a member of the World Society for the Protection of Animals, as he rescues animals in danger, such as from floods.

Gross, Virginia T. *The Day It Rained Forever: A Story of the Johnstown Flood*. New York: Viking, 1991. In this novel, Christina and her family are living in Johnstown, Pennsylvania, when the dam bursts.

Hiscock, Bruce. *The Big Rivers: The Missouri, the Mississippi, and the Ohio*. New York: Athenaeum Books for Young Readers, 1997. Hiscock explains the vast flooding of the Midwestern United States in 1993.

Kehret, Peg. *The Flood Disaster*. New York: Simon & Schuster, 1999. Warren and Betsy travel back in time to Johnstown, Pennsylvania, in 1889.

Lauber, Patricia. *Flood: Wrestling with the Mississippi*. Washington, DC: National Geographic Society, 1996. Lauber provides a photo essay of the 1993 Mississippi River flood in the Midwestern United States.

Spilsbury, Louise. *Raging Floods*. Chicago: Heinemann Library, 2003. This book explains what causes floods and how they can be prevented.

Woods, Michael, and Mary B. Woods. *Hurricanes*. Minneapolis: Lerner Publications, 2007.

Woods, Michael, and Mary B. Woods. *Tsunamis*. Minneapolis: Lerner Publications, 2007.

WEBSITES & FILMS

Basics of Flooding

http://www.floodplain.org/flood_basics.htm

Find out about the basics of flooding and flood protection at this site sponsored by the Floodplain Management Association.

Emergency Management Agency for Kids

http://ema.ohio.gov/kids_page/

The Ohio Department of Public Safety sponsors this site to help teach about the natural disasters that occur in Ohio.

Eye in the Sky: Floods and Dams

http://www.nationalgeographic.com/eye/floods/effect.html

Sponsored by the National Geographic Society, this site provides videos of deforestation, a slow-moving flood, and people moving their possessions during a flood.

FEMA

http://www.fema.gov/

This is the site for the Federal Emergency Management Agency, the main U.S. government agency that fights floods.

Flash Flood!

http://noaa.kids.us/flashflo.htm

The National Weather Service sponsors this site with Owlie Skywarn giving safety tips.

The Hows and Whys of Floods

http://www.pbs.org/newshour/infocus/floods/science.html

View this site to find out about El Niño and floods, sponsored by PBS.

Modern Wonders: The Aswan High Dam

http://ce.eng.usf.edu/pharos/wonders/Modern/aswandam.html

This site explains how and why the Aswan Dam was built.

National Weather Service Hydrologic Information Center: Flood Summary

http://www.nws.noaa.gov/oh/hic/current/fln/fln_sum.shtml

The National Weather Service updates this site daily with the latest news about flood conditions around the United States.

Natural Hazards: Causes and Effects: Lesson 6: Floods

http://dmc.engr.wisc.edu/courses/hazards/BB02-06.html

The University of Wisconsin sponsors this site to teach about floods.

The 1953 East Coast Floods

http://www.bbc.co.uk/weather/features/understanding/1953_flood.shtml

In 1953 a flood caused by a strong storm surge devastated the east coast of England.

NOAA Center for Tsunami Research

http://nctr.pmel.noaa.gov/

Find out about the various tsunami warning systems.

Online Disaster Quiz

http://www.redcross.org/news/dro/game.html

Take this disaster quiz to test your knowledge of how to remain safe.

Preparedness Today: What You Need to Do

http://www.redcross.org/disaster/disasterguide/standardmsg.html

The Coalition of Organizations for Disaster Education has updated its guide for standardized disaster warning messages.

Story of the Great Flood and Cyclone Disaster

http://www.usgennet.org/usa/topic/preservation/nature/flood/chpt2a.htm

Read about the flood of 1913 in Ohio and Indiana.

Survivors Remember Flood as If It Happened Yesterday
http://www.pittsburghlive.com/x/tribune-review/regional/s_81290.html
Read stories from flood survivors in Tanneryville, Pennsylvania.

Tsunami!
http://www.geophys.washington.edu/tsunami/welcome.html
This site was developed at the University of Washington to provide general information about tsunamis.

WeatherEye
http://weathereye.kgan.com/cadet/index.html
Central Iowa Power Cooperative (CIPCO) sponsors this site to help you learn about various types of weather.

Flash Floods: Deadly Downpour. New York: History Channel. 2001. The title from the Wrath of God series takes a look at extremely dangerous flash floods.

Flood! Boston: NOVA, 1996. See actual footage of the Mississippi River flood of 1993.

Floods. Wynnewood, PA: Schlessinger Videos, 2003. This video explores the role that climate and geography play in causing floods in certain geographic areas.

Hurricane Katrina: The Storm That Drowned a City. Boston: NOVA, 2005. The entire Gulf Coast area of the United States is vulnerable to flooding because of the destruction of its natural marsh areas. This video includes some actual footage of the flooding in New Orleans in 2005.

Tsunami: The Wave That Shook the World. Boston: NOVA, 2005. See actual footage of the flooding that occurred after the December 26, 2004, tsunami struck land surrounding the Indian Ocean.

Index

Photo Acknowledgments

The images in this book are used with the permission of: © Steve Johnson, p. 1; © Getty Images, pp. 3, 5, 15, 17, 20, 26, 27, 35, 37, 38, 39 (both), 46, 47, 51, 53, 55 (bottom); © ARKO DATTA/Reuters/CORBIS, p. 4; © Nimatallah/Art Resource, NY, p. 7; © Liu Liqun/CORBIS, p. 9; © Bettmann/CORBIS, pp. 10, 55 (top); AP Images/Jeff Pruyne, p. 11; National Oceanic and Atmospheric Administration Central Library Photo Collection, pp. 12, 18, 21, 50; © North Wind Picture Archives, p. 13; Library of Congress, p. 19 (LC-USZ62-8685); AP Images/Eugene Hoshiko, p. 22; Patsy Lynch/FEMA, p. 23; U.S. Geological Survey/photo by R. R. Shroba, p. 24; U.S. Geological Survey/photo by W. R. Hansen, p. 25 (both); Andrea Booher/FEMA, p. 30; © Najlah Feanny/CORBIS, p. 31 (top); © Andrew Holbrooke/CORBIS, p. 31 (bottom); © Bob Landry/Time Life Pictures/Getty Images, p. 33; © RAFIQUR RAHMAN/Reuters/CORBIS, p. 34; © epa/CORBIS, p. 36; U.S. Army Corps of Engineers, p. 41; © China Photo/Reuters/CORBIS, p. 42; © PUNIT PARANJPE/Reuters/CORBIS, p. 43; © Reuters/CORBIS, p. 45; David Saville/FEMA, p. 49; © Alessandro della Bella/epa/CORBIS, p. 52; © Mary Evans Picture Library/The Image Works, p. 54.

Front Cover: © Marko Georgiev/Getty Images; Back Cover: Library of Congress (LC-DIG-ggbain-12012)

About the Authors

Michael Woods is a science and medical journalist in Washington, D.C., who has won many national writing awards. Mary B. Woods is a school librarian. Their past books include the eight-volume Ancient Technology series. The Woods have four children. When not writing, reading, or enjoying their grandchildren, the Woods travel to gather material for future books.